HISTORIC PHOTOS OF
THE PRESIDIO

TEXT AND CAPTIONS BY REBECCA SCHALL

TURNER
PUBLISHING COMPANY

Originally constructed for the 1915 Panama-Pacific Exposition on designs by Bernard
Maybeck, the Palace of Fine Arts is situated on the grounds of the San Francisco Presidio,
today part of the Golden Gate National Recreation Area.

HISTORIC PHOTOS OF
THE PRESIDIO

Turner Publishing Company
200 4th Avenue North • Suite 950
Nashville, Tennessee 37219
(615) 255-2665

Historic Photos of the Presidio

www.turnerpublishing.com

Library of Congress Control Number: 2008901851

ISBN-13: 978-1-59652-444-6

Printed in the United States of America

08 09 10 11 12 13 14 15—0 9 8 7 6 5 4 3 2 1

CONTENTS

The Alameda of the Presidio is shown here in the early twentieth century. The Alameda was the formal road leading to the Parade Grounds.

Acknowledgments

Thank you to my family—Fran Schall, Gerald Schall, Teddy Schall, and Pedie Schall. I am reminded every day how lucky I am because of you.

Thank you to the San Francisco Public Library; the Library of Congress; the Golden Gate National Recreation Area, Park Archives; and Amanda Williford from the Presidio Archive.

———————

For my grandfathers,
Harry Schall (February 23, 1914–June 20, 2008) and Samuel Berger (January 6, 1916–June 13, 2001),
both of whom served overseas in the U.S. Army during World War II and loved San Francisco

PREFACE

The Presidio is a National Park in the Golden Gate National Recreation Area and a National Historic Landmark, spanning nearly 1,500 acres in the heart of San Francisco. The commonly fog-swathed Presidio has a far-reaching cultural history extending back thousands of years to the indigenous Native American tribes that lived in the Bay Area. Archaeologists have uncovered extensive evidence of the inhabitations of the Presidio coastline by the Ohlone people.

The Presidio, Spanish for "fortress," has been a military bastion of enormous national and international importance. Over the course of three centuries here, three flags have been flown—first those of Spain and Mexico, and from 1846 forward, the Stars and Stripes of the United States.

The Presidio has been home to famous American generals, including William Tecumseh Sherman, George Henry Thomas, and John J. Pershing. It played a leading role in America's chief military engagements throughout the nineteenth and twentieth centuries. Most prominently, it was the point of embarkation in 1898 for American troops fighting in the Philippines during the Spanish-American War, America's first conflict in the Asian Pacific. During World War II, it served as the center of defense for the American West. Executive Order 9066, interning Americans of Japanese descent, was signed in the Presidio in 1942.

The Presidio housed a large army hospital from the 1890s onward, renamed the Letterman Army Medical Center in 1911, which treated hundreds of thousands of wounded soldiers during every major conflict of the late nineteenth and twentieth centuries. Over the century and a half that the Presidio has been part of the United States, it has given rise to ground-breaking military hospitals, airfields, and a vast innovative coastal defense system. Over the same period, its landscape evolved from a barren, windswept expanse of sand dunes and coastal shrubs into a luxuriant forest. Today the Presidio is known for its scenic landscape, verdant forests, and historic architecture spanning several hundred years.

On October 1, 1994, the soldiers of the Sixth Army marched out of the gates of the Presidio, marking its close as a military base. Today, hikers enjoy the Presidio, incorporated into the Golden Gate National Recreation Area, a series of parks administered by the National Park Service throughout the San Francisco Bay Area. Since 1998, the Presidio Trust has overseen the preservation and administration of the buildings and landscape of the Presidio, which is on the verge of becoming the first financially self-sustaining national park in the country.

When photography emerged in the nineteenth century, the contemporary world could be documented in unprecedented ways. Thousands of photographs of the Presidio were recorded, many ending up in archives. While those photographs are of great interest to many, they are not always easily accessible. This book is the result of countless hours of reviewing thousands of photos in the San Francisco Public Library Archives and the Archive and Record Center of the Presidio, as well as extensive historical research. I greatly appreciate the generous assistance of Amanda Williford at the Archive and Record Center of the Presidio and others listed in the acknowledgments of this work, without whom this book could not have been possible.

The goal in publishing this work is to provide broader access to these historic photographs, thereby helping to preserve the story of this American landmark with proper respect and reverence. The photographs selected have been reproduced in their original black-and-white format to provide depth to the images. With the exception of touching up imperfections caused by the damage of time and cropping where necessary, no other alterations have been made.

This book is divided into five sections, delineating key eras in the history of the Presidio. Section One looks at the Presidio in the second half of the nineteenth century, as the land was transformed from barren, wind-swept coastal bluffs into a lush forest, and as the Presidio evolved into a strong and bustling American military base as a result of America's involvement in the Spanish-American War. The second section explores the Presidio between 1900 and 1919, including its role in helping the city of San Francisco recover from the devastation of the 1906 earthquake and fires. Section Three covers the Presidio in the 1920s and 1930s, during the interwar period and the building of pioneering Crissy Airfield. Section Four captures the Presidio's boom years during World War II, when it returned to center-stage in world affairs and served as a hub for assembling, training, and the embarkation of troops fighting in the Pacific theater of the war. Section Five surveys the postwar period, when the Presidio served as base for the Sixth Army and as a center for Nike missile activity during the cold war.

In each section, *Historic Photos of the Presidio* attempts to capture various aspects of life in the Presidio during these periods and the rich layers of history of this National Historic Landmark. I encourage readers to reflect appreciatively on the momentous history and beauty of this urban treasure.

—*Rebecca Schall*

A Regimental Review is pictured on the Presidio grounds in 1900 following the Spanish-American War. Secretary of State John Hay called the conflict with Spain a "splendid little war," because America emerged as an imperial power at the start of the twentieth century, with colonies on both sides of the globe, including the Philippines, Guam, and Puerto Rico.

THE GARRISON COMES OF AGE

(1870s–1899)

The Ohlone Indians lived along the shores of what is the Presidio for thousands of years before the first European on record, Don Gaspar de Portola, discovered San Francisco Bay in 1769. Spain had urged the colonization of the areas north of their existing "New Spain" settlements (in today's Mexico and Southern California) in efforts to establish Spanish territory in the face of encroaching English and Russian settlements on the Pacific coastline. In 1776, Juan Bautista de Anza led an expedition of 193 colonists, including Spanish missionaries, soldiers, forty families, and more than a thousand cattle from northern Mexico, settling at the mouth of the bay in what would become the Presidio. There, they established their first settlement, el Presidio de San Francisco, a garrison composed of a small quadrangle, which would gradually expand over the decades. Several miles inland, the Spanish established Mission San Francisco de Assisi, today known as Mission Dolores. The Presidio, Mission Dolores, and the nearby pueblo of Yerba Buena formed the beginnings of what would evolve into the modern city of San Francisco, but which remained the detached northernmost outpost of New Spain for the next half-century.

When Mexico gained independence from Spain in 1821, San Francisco became part of Mexico's quiet Alta California province, and the people of the Presidio switched their allegiance from the Spanish to the Mexican flag. By 1835, most of the families living in the Presidio moved 50 miles north to Sonoma under the command of General Mariano Vallejo to quell a possible advance by the Russians of Fort Ross into Alta California territory. During this time, the Presidio, handed to a caretaker, declined in military importance and fell into a state of decay.

In 1846, American forces occupied the Presidio during the Mexican War. That same year, American soldiers and renegades in Sonoma revolted against Mexican rule in the Bear Flag Rebellion, and John Fremont sailed across the Golden Gate to declare the Presidio part of the newly established Bear Flag Republic. As a consequence of the Mexican War and the Treaty of Guadalupe Hidalgo, the Presidio was handed over to the jurisdiction of the United States. The following year, American settlers occupying the pueblo of Yerba Buena renamed the town San Francisco. During this time, the dilapidated adobe structures of the Presidio were repaired by the U.S. Army.

After the discovery of gold at Sutter's Mill in the Sierra foothills of California in 1848, fortune hunters and adventurers the world over rushed to California in one of the greatest human migrations in history. In 1850, as California joined the Union to become the 31st state, San Francisco, its population exploding, was becoming a melting pot in which people from distant lands, distinct traditions, different political views, and varied ways of life lived and worked together. This dramatic increase in population required a military presence, and in November 1850, President Millard Fillmore designated the San Francisco Presidio a military base.

During the Gold Rush, San Francisco emerged as the mining capital of the West and the state's center for commerce and the press. California's factories, banks, and other businesses prospered in San Francisco in the early years of statehood. As a result of its sundry population, San Francisco acquired a cosmopolitan flavor, and the attitudes of its citizens were often as varied as the cities from which they came.

San Francisco's strategic position on the West Coast meant that it could help defend and protect the entire nation, and the Presidio was charged with that role. The garrison's position at the mouth of the Bay enabled it to protect the city from invasion. In 1853, construction began on Fort Point, an imposing granite and brick fortress with six-foot-thick walls and built to hold 126 cannons.

With the outbreak of the Civil War in 1861, the Presidio became an important center of defense and began once again to expand its acreage. During the second half of the nineteenth century, soldiers in the Presidio played pivotal roles fighting in the Indian wars of the American West. In the 1880s, a massive tree-planting and beautification project took hold, transforming the landscape over the next century from barren sand dunes to a verdant forest of eucalyptus, cypress, and pine. The U.S. Cavalry of the Presidio was put in charge of maintaining parks and resources, and spent summers patrolling and maintaining monuments such as Sequoia and Yosemite national parks. In the late 1800s and early 1900s, many coastal defense batteries were built along the bluffs in the western Presidio.

In 1898, the Spanish-American War broke out, making San Francisco the most important military base in the West. Thousands of troops camped here as they awaited embarkation to the Philippines, and thousands of wounded soldiers returned here for treatment in the U.S. Army General Hospital built in 1899. By the end of the nineteenth century, the Presidio was no longer an isolated and neglected outpost, but a massive military base of central importance to the defense of the United States.

The Presidio is pictured here on July 3, 1876, during a mock battle at Harbor View. During the mid–nineteenth century, Harbor View was built by Rudolph Hermann near the current intersection of Jefferson and Baker streets as a public resort. One hundred years earlier, at the time of Spanish colonization in California, the Presidio, the mission, and the nearby pueblo constituted the Spanish strategy. Presidios were armed military bases that established order. The pueblos were villages of colonists that spread Spanish culture. The missions were religious centers designed to spread Catholicism to the native people and convert them into loyal Catholic subjects of the Spanish crown. The San Francisco Presidio's purpose was to have jurisdiction over the native population and to capture native Indians who escaped the mission, as well as to safeguard the area from foreign intruders. During the Spanish period and the subsequent Mexican period, the San Francisco Presidio helped create four pueblos, five missions, and many ranches throughout the Bay Area. Owing to its position on the periphery of the Spanish frontier, supplies and provisions at the Presidio of San Francisco were almost always inadequate. The city of San Francisco was then known as Yerba Buena, after the fragrant herb abundant in the area.

The Presidio has changed considerably since the nineteenth century, as seen in this photograph from 1883. Before humans arrived in the area thousands of years ago, the Presidio looked very different from its appearance today. Ten thousand years ago, the shoreline was located twenty miles to the west. The coastal bluffs held a great diversity of flora and fauna. Grizzly bears, mountain lions, bobcats, wolves, elk, and antelope roamed the shoreline, and bald eagles soared overhead.

The Presidio and the drive to Fort Point in the 1880s are shown here. The Presidio was originally a windswept land of sand dunes, grasslands, and coastal shrubs. The thin, dry soil had little potential for agriculture, nor forage for cattle, yet the Spanish soon claimed the coastal lands to raise their cattle and to grow food. The cows and sheep that the Spanish brought with them carried the seeds of exotic flora, which gradually led to the proliferation of non-native plant species. Today, the 800 acres of open space in the Presidio, including the historic 300-acre forest, is home to many rare and endangered species like the California quail, coyote, gray fox, and numerous intertidal species along the shoreline. The Presidio also boasts many native species that have gone virtually extinct in the rest of the Bay Area, including 300 native species of flora.

A horse and carriage travel a winding road leading to the Presidio's Alameda entrance in the late nineteenth century. The Alameda (Spanish for "avenue") was the main entrance to the Presidio from the 1860s until 1895. During this period, cannonballs edged the streets in a decorative manner, and soldiers guarded the entrance. This entrance, close to the current intersection of Presidio Boulevard and Funston Avenue, no longer exists.

The main parade grounds of the Presidio are shown here in the 1890s. The Presidio was the size of a small city. Today, the Presidio has almost 800 buildings, nearly 500 of which are of historic significance. For this reason, the Presidio has been designated a National Historic Landmark District. The layers of diverse architectural styles spanning four centuries reflect the Presidio's transformation into a garrison of national and international significance. Architectural styles include Greek revival (1840-1860), Italianate (1860-1880), Queen Anne (1880-1890), colonial revival (1880-1940), mission revival (1910-1940), Mediterranean and Italian Renaissance revival (1920-1940), World War II, postwar, and modern era (1945-present), utilitarian styles (1860-present), and various eclectic anomalies.

A woman stands in the Presidio in the late nineteenth century. During the Spanish period, from 1776 to 1821, the Presidio protected the Bay from infringing foreign powers. In the early years, the native Ohlone cohabited with Europeans and the colonists from Mexico, who had mixed Spanish, native, and African ancestry. Colonists at the Presidio spent their days farming, transforming the landscape, and converting the native people to Catholicism. The Presidio and Alta California had an economy based on the trade of seal and otter fur, and the hides and tallow of cattle.

Soldiers fire cannons in the Presidio in the late nineteenth century. In the 1820s, news of Mexico's independence took twelve months to reach the Presidio. Once it did, little changed, except the change of allegiance from Spanish to Mexican flags. Under Mexican rule, many of the former Presidio soldiers and settlers founded cattle and horse ranches, and created a society known as Californio, often becoming very wealthy and living very luxurious lives. The native populations were forever affected by Spanish colonization and subsequent Mexican rule. Their ancestral lands were turned into rancheros, and their traditional way of life and culture destroyed. During the Mexican period, many surviving Ohlone Indians became vaqueros, or cowboys, and peons in pueblos and on rancheros.

This late-nineteenth-century photograph, found in the Long Family Album, shows a young girl standing alone with her dog. Most army officers based at the Presidio lived comfortably with their families on the grounds and enjoyed their time on the base. Children went to school there, and most of the military families' interaction was with other military families.

The Long family enjoys a leisurely picnic in the Presidio on a spring day in the late nineteenth century.

The Long family at home, with climbing roses and other vines trimming their Presidio landscape.

Several generations of the Long family gather on the front steps of their home on Officers Row.

The Longs enjoy the moment
outside their home in the Presidio.

A woman putts at the Presidio Golf Course. When it was built in 1895, this 9-hole course was one of the first golf courses on the West Coast. The course was used during the Spanish-American War for military training, although it remained open for recreational purposes.

Children play in front of well-maintained two-story homes along Officers Row in the Presidio. During the late 1880s and 1890s, these homes, built decades earlier along Funston Avenue on the Presidio grounds, were refurbished extensively, and new quarters were constructed nearby to accommodate additional officers and their families.

A soldier based in the Presidio gazes toward his wife in the late nineteenth century as she sits atop a field howitzer dating back to the Civil War.

Five soldiers pose outside their tent at the Presidio in 1898 during the Spanish-American War. America declared war on April 21, 1898, after the explosion of the USS *Maine* in the harbor of Havana, Cuba, and because America supported Cuba's independence from Spain. This was the first overseas conflict the United States had faced, and its first battle would take place in the Pacific in another Spanish colony fighting for independence—the Philippines. Under Commodore George Dewey, the U.S. Navy defeated the Spanish fleet at Manila Bay on May 1, sustaining but a single casualty. Meanwhile, President McKinley recruited volunteer troops to embark on a campaign against the Filipino capital at Manila. Thousands of these volunteers lived temporarily in tents on the eastern part of the Presidio, where they went through extensive training.

This 1898 image shows tents in the foreground erected for troops during the Spanish-American War, and Alcatraz in the background. The San Francisco Presidio was the ideal point of embarkation for the Philippines because of its locale along the best natural harbor on the Pacific coast of California, and because of the large tract of land there that could accommodate thousands of troops. During the war, 80,000 troops, the majority of those who fought in the Philippines, came through the Presidio on their way to the Pacific. Just behind the tents stand the "30th Infantry Barracks," which faced the main parade ground. Alcatraz, the first army post built on the Pacific Coast (Fort Point and the fortifications on Angel Island were begun the same year), was occupied by several artillery detachments in 1898. The sudden influx of tens of thousands of troops required rapid expansion and improvement of the Presidio. New buildings were constructed all over the grounds, including the Letterman Hospital and the Montgomery Street Barracks. The war catapulted the Presidio from a frontier army post to preeminence as a modern American army base.

This photograph, taken during the Spanish-American War, was titled "The Last General Inspection Before Embarkation." By the time most of the troops arrived in the Philippines from the Presidio, the war with Spain was nearly over, but a new conflict was beginning between Filipino nationalists and the United States—the Philippine Insurrection or Philippine-American War. Nationalists, led by Emilio Aguinaldo, were infuriated when the United States wanted to take the Philippines as its own colony after the war with Spain, instead of granting it the independence it sought from Spain. At first, Aguinaldo's 40,000 nationals far outnumbered the American soldiers, but eventually, 75,000 Americans were deployed to fight there.

Shown in this 1897 image is the Presidio Avenue Gate. The straight path at center is the historic "Lovers Lane." In the background is the site of the present Fort Winfield Scott, Fort Point, and the southern anchorage of the Golden Gate Bridge. Across the Bay, to the right, is Fort Baker, named in honor of Colonel Edward Dickinson Baker (the "Gray Eagle"). Troops drawn up before the gate are part of the detachment stationed at the Presidio at the time.

Volunteer soldiers from across the country came to the Presidio and joined those already stationed at the base. The 51st Iowa Volunteer Infantry Regiment is pictured marching out of the Lombard Gate as the soldiers leave for the Philippines in 1898. A stone monument was placed in the Presidio on the site where the 51st was camped prior to shipping out. The Lombard Gate, constructed in 1896, was the main entrance to the Presidio during the Spanish-American War, and it was the gate through which the majority of troops fighting in the Philippines passed. The sandstone gate, decorated with cannons and other military designs, helped delineate the Presidio boundaries and beautify this approach to the city of San Francisco.

Soldiers for the Spanish-American War pose for a group shot while lounging in their tents. The caption accompanying the original photograph says "wouldn't get up for roll call." Typically, six to eight volunteer soldiers were crammed into each tent on the Presidio grounds. The tight living quarters and unhealthful conditions led to frequent maladies among the volunteers.

A Presidio cook detail stands behind steaming cookpots during the Spanish-American War. Volunteer soldiers were very well fed while stationed on the grounds.

Pictured here is the 9th Cavalry Band of the celebrated Buffalo Soldiers, just before leaving for China in 1900. Buffalo Soldiers were the all African-American 9th and 10th Cavalry, and 24th and 25th Infantry regiments that helped settle the American frontier. The sobriquet "Buffalo Soldiers" is believed to have come from the western Plains Indians, who respected these soldiers as worthy opponents for their courage and ferocity in battle and believed that their dark hair bore a resemblance to the fur between the horns on a buffalo's head.

Buffalo Soldiers stand in the Presidio before shipping out to fight in the Spanish-American War. The buffalo symbol later became part of the crest of the 10th Cavalry Regiment. Buffalo Soldiers played an integral role in settling the American West, as well as fighting for the American cause abroad.

In the late nineteenth and early twentieth centuries, the Buffalo Soldiers of the 24th Infantry and the 9th Cavalry were stationed in the Presidio. Despite the meritorious role they played in the United States Army, the Buffalo Soldiers were garrisoned in segregated units. The men who served in these units are respected for their courage and patriotism, as well as for their efforts to surmount the hardship of discrimination in the United States against African-Americans at the time.

An artillery drill at the Presidio is pictured in this postcard image from around 1900.

THE GREAT EARTHQUAKE AND THE GREAT WAR

(1900–1919)

In the half-century following the Gold Rush, San Francisco transformed from a sleepy trading town into the widely heralded "Paris of the West." Once a small hamlet with fewer than 700 people in the late 1840s, San Francisco's population had swelled to around 400,000 by the early 1900s, making it the ninth-largest city in the nation.

In 1903, President Theodore Roosevelt visited San Francisco and was escorted by an honor guard composed of the Presidio's 10th Cavalry Regiment, one of several units of the Buffalo Soldiers, who had played a strong role in the charge up San Juan Hill during the Spanish-American War. By 1905, the soldiers of the Presidio had built a dozen reinforced concrete batteries for coastal defense. The entire coastline was guarded by Presidio coastal artillery units, as well as cavalry and infantry.

While buoyant optimism marked the initial years of the 1900s in San Francisco, the euphoria was short-lived. Disaster struck early on the morning of April 18, 1906, when the San Andreas Fault ruptured. The city sustained the largest earthquake the nation had seen, estimated as high as 8.3 on the Richter Scale. What the earthquake and aftershocks did not reduce to rubble, the fires that followed destroyed. Separate blazes that ignited in the immediate aftermath of the earthquake converged into one massive inferno, ultimately destroying more than 500 city blocks, with firemen helpless to extinguish it and leaving more than two-thirds of the population homeless. The earthquake and fires of 1906 were the most significant event in San Francisco's history, and one of the nation's worst urban disasters.

Under the direction of General Frederick Funston, recipient of the Medal of Honor for his bravery in the Philippines, the U.S. Army of the Presidio played a pivotal role in helping the devastated city recover. Presidio soldiers offered clothing, food, and shelter for the people of San Francisco and reestablished law and order during the chaos that followed the event. Thousands of the city's new homeless camped out in tent cities in the Presidio.

The Presidio experienced many other significant developments in the early twentieth century. In 1911, the U.S. Army General Hospital was renamed Letterman Army Hospital, after Jonathan Letterman, who had served in all major military engagements in the twentieth century up to that time. In 1912, Fort Winfield Scott was completed in the western Presidio as the headquarters of the Artillery District of San Francisco to help oversee the West Coast's vast coastal defense system. In 1916, General John J. Pershing organized a mission to Mexico to suppress the forces of Pancho Villa, the Mexican rebel and outlaw who led raids across the Mexican border into the United States. While Pershing headed up the Mexican Expedition, his family was killed in a fire in their house in the Presidio. This led to the establishment of the Presidio Fire Department, the first 24-hour fire station on a military base. Pershing would go on to become Commander of the American Expeditionary Forces in Europe during World War I and Chief of Staff of the Army.

After almost a decade of rapid rebuilding, a revitalized San Francisco celebrated its renaissance in the Panama-Pacific International Exposition in 1915, which was partially located on the Presidio waterfront on the border of the Marina District. The exposition officially recognized the completion of the Panama Canal, Teddy Roosevelt's feat of engineering that substantially shortened the time required to reach San Francisco from points east by ship. More than anything else, the exposition paid tribute to the old city lost in the quake and celebrated the rebirth, recovery, and endurance of a magnificent new San Francisco. Part of the Bay was filled in for construction of the exposition grounds. Presidio soldiers participated in the exposition with parades, honor guards, and artillery shows.

With America's entry into World War I in 1917, the Presidio built new training areas and became an important recruiting and training center for American soldiers who were to fight in the war in Europe. The Presidio also had an officer's training camp and was bustling with army traffic for the duration of the war. The San Francisco–based 30th Infantry Regiment earned acclaim fighting in World War I, to become known as the "Rock of the Marne." From 1918 to 1920, the little-known American Expeditionary Force Siberia was created and trained in the Presidio. The force was dispatched to Siberia during the Russian Civil War, suffering 189 casualties over its 19-month mission. On November 11, 1918, with the end of the First World War, returning soldiers marched down San Francisco's Market Street in a victory parade, and the city looked ahead to a new era of peace and good fortune, owing in no small way to the existence and exploits of the Presidio.

The Presidio and Ferries Railroad 28, shown here in the Presidio in 1900, opened cable car service on January 1, 1882, along Union Street, extending the cable car line westward into the Presidio in the early 1890s.

Many of the fallen and wounded soldiers were sent home to the Presidio after fighting in the Philippines. A military funeral procession makes its way along the main parade grounds in the Presidio in the early 1900s. Because of the large number of war casualties, the San Francisco National Cemetery, founded in the Presidio in 1884, was enlarged.

Garrison prisoners helped distribute the million pounds of coal brought each month into the Presidio with mules and carts.

Pictured here in the early 1900s is the Municipal Railways Presidio Terminal, with its covered platform, waiting room, and track loop.

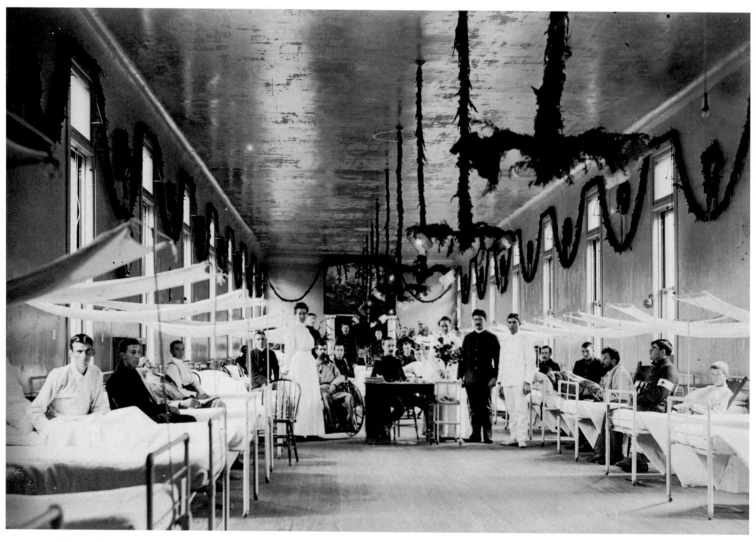

A hospital ward at the Letterman Army Hospital, shown here in 1902. Letterman was built in 1898 and given its name in 1911, in honor of Jonathan Letterman. This hospital served a prominent role in the Spanish-American War, World War I, World War II, the Korean War, and the Vietnam War. It was razed in the 1960s and replaced with a modern hospital in 1969. The new hospital was abandoned 25 years later when the Presidio was handed over to the National Park Service, and has now been replaced with Lucasfilm's new Letterman Digital Arts Center, which opened on the former site of the original hospital in 2005.

A Letterman Hospital nurse stands beneath fanciful light fixtures in this image from the early 1900s.

Decades before the Golden Gate Bridge was built, Fort Point stands solitary watch over the Bay. Situated at the mouth of the Golden Gate, this Civil War–era fortress protected San Francisco Bay from Confederate attack during the Civil War and foreign attack afterward. Its seven-foot-thick walls and multi-tiered casemated construction were state-of-the-art when construction began in 1853. As plans for the Golden Gate Bridge were devised in the 1930s, city officials favored demolishing the obsolete fort, but the bridge's chief engineer, Joseph Strauss, reconfigured the plans to save the historic fort. Alfred Hitchcock fans know Fort Point as the place where Jimmy Stewart saved Kim Novak from drowning in the chilly Pacific waters in the classic film *Vertigo*. Fort Point is now a protected National Historic Site, and visitors can admire its arched casemates and brick masonry as guides in Civil War–period costume bring the fort's military history to life.

On April 18, 1906, a severe earthquake struck San Francisco. The Presidio played a leading role in helping San Franciscans by setting up refugee camps and supplying emergency supplies and food. Its soldiers also helped keep law and order throughout the city. The fires that burned for three days after the temblor did far more damage than the quake itself. The earthquake knocked out transportation lines, telephone lines, and water mains. Efforts to extinguish the fires were futile. Of 400,000 citizens, more than 250,000 were left homeless, and 28,000 buildings were reduced to rubble. Damages were sustained in excess of $50 billion in today's currency. The 1906 earthquake was the first disaster of this magnitude to be captured by photography, enabling people all over the world to see the devastation. A group of cavalrymen are shown in the Presidio in 1906, shortly after the earthquake and fires.

Earthquake refugees are pictured here leaving the Presidio landing in 1906. While the official death toll following the earthquake and fires tallied fewer than 400, researchers believe that more than 3,000 people perished, and that casualties were deliberately understated to protect real estate prices and encourage investors to finance the rebuilding of the city.

After the quake, the Presidio and Golden Gate Park were turned into refugee camps. The largest camp on the Presidio grounds is shown here, with the United States Army General Hospital in the background.

Seen here is a bread line at one of the camps on the Presidio grounds. After the earthquake, the U.S. Army responded quickly to the immediate needs of the devastated city. Within days, forces stationed at the Presidio supplied 3,000 tents, 13,000 ponchos, 58,000 pairs of shoes, 24,000 shirts, and 20,000 blankets, as well as large quantities of bread baked by the Presidio bakery.

After the 1906 earthquake, the Presidio provided food and shelter to thousands of refugees. San Francisco itself was divided into military districts protected by the soldiers, and Presidio soldiers oversaw the 21 refugee camps that sprang up around the city. The 3,000 tents in the Presidio refugee camp were organized into a grid, with street numbers and signs. Medical personnel on duty in the Presidio helped ensure sanitation to prevent disease outbreaks, and soldiers carefully patrolled and cared for the refugees. The four camps in the Presidio were the first in the city to close in June. Many of the temporary wood cottages were purchased by refugees who lived there and moved into parts of the city afterward. The camps, established and overseen by the Presidio, helped thousands survive the devastation and regain their lives.

A crowd of civilians and soldiers gather at the water barrel camp after the 1906 earthquake.

A scene of everyday life in the Presidio's tent city for earthquake refugees. This pair makes do at a makeshift camp table outside their tent.

Children stand in front of their refugee camp in the Presidio. San Francisco Mayor Eugene Schmitz issued a "shoot to kill" order against all looters and troublemakers following the disaster, and Presidio troops were posted along Market Street and throughout the city to establish order. Troops also assisted injured citizens, distributed food and supplies, and helped fight the fires.

Construction of temporary shelter in the Presidio is under way following the earthquake. Amid the city's smoldering ruins, imagining that San Francisco could not only be rebuilt but also thrive again would have been difficult. San Franciscans nevertheless immediately began a massive rebuilding project. Like the phoenix, that mythical bird which rose from the ashes of its death, San Francisco wanted to become the world-class city it had been, even more spectacular than before. By 1907, scant months after the disaster, San Franciscans proclaimed that the city was open for business. Within several years, nearly 20,000 new buildings would be added to city streets.

The boardwalk to Fort Point from the entrance to the Presidio at Presidio Avenue is shown here in 1908. During the eighteenth century, this foot path, known as Lover's Lane, was a road that passed through the Tennessee Hollow Watershed in the Presidio, connecting the Presidio to the pueblo of Yerba Buena. It was mostly used at that time by Spanish soldiers and missionaries as a direct path to Mission Dolores, three miles inland, but in the nineteenth century, it was the path to town used by off-duty American soldiers.

The 30th U.S. Infantry is shown here in 1910 engaged in military maneuvers near Baker Beach, a pristine beach that is part of the Presidio reservation.

The guns of the Presidio are shown here in April 1908.

The Lombard Gate, showing the Quartermaster storehouses and sentry on duty, is pictured here in 1912.

A panorama of construction of the main exhibit palaces of the Panama-Pacific International Exposition of 1915, as seen from the Presidio. The 635-acre exposition officially recognized the completion of the Panama Canal and paid tribute to the old San Francisco lost in the earthquake of 1906. Presidio soldiers participated in the exposition with parades, honor guards, and artillery shows.

Pictured here is a U.S. Army supply wagon at the Presidio, Sixteenth Infantry Company L.

Soldiers compete in a tug of war at the Presidio. Shortly after this photo was shot, Company B won the contest.

The wood construction and coal-burning fireplaces in buildings in the Presidio left them vulnerable to fire. While Presidio commander General John J. Pershing was in search of the Mexican outlaw Pancho Villa in 1916, his house caught fire from coal falling from the fireplace in the dining room, killing his wife and three of his four children. In this photo, fire fighters work aggressively to extinguish the fire at General Pershing's residence. This tragedy led to a Congressional mandate to significantly improve fire safety at the military reservation. In 1917, the Army built a permanent Presidio fire station, with trained fire fighters ready to respond at a moment's notice, 24 hours a day. With American entry into World War I, General Pershing became Commander of the American Expeditionary Forces in Europe.

Private George E. Maker poses on horseback in the Presidio in 1915. Halim, a purebreed Arabian stallion, was owned by Major James G. Harford, the First U.S. Cavalry commanding officer based in the Presidio.

An early aviator poses in his airplane along the Presidio waterfront in 1915.

Soldiers skirmish in mock combat around 1917-18 at the reservation.

Following Spread: The Presidio's Company E is being reviewed.

The Presidio Golf Club is pictured here in the early twentieth century. In addition to providing a place of recreation for Presidio officers, it served as a training site for troops being sent to fight in the Spanish-American War, and a refugee camp for those made homeless in the 1906 earthquake. The 9-hole course was converted to 18-hole in 1910, and after the Presidio closed as an Army base, the course was opened to the public.

Two soldiers ride horses in the Presidio in a "Monkey Drill," a mounted drill routine requiring troops to ride without a saddle while putting the horse through various maneuvers.

The Presidio's collection of weaponry has included old cannons, two of them shown here outside the reservation's museum. Among the cannons are six Spanish models dating from the seventeenth century, among the oldest artillery in North America, including El Birgen de Barbaneda, which was cast in Peru in 1693.

Garrison soldiers are shown here peeling potatoes around 1918.

Coastal artillery troops parade past their Montgomery Street barracks in the Presidio as officers observe. Built of brick in the 1890s in the colonial revival style, the barracks, referred to as "Infantry Row," housed enlisted soldiers for decades.

Soldiers of the 30th Regiment gather at an athletic field in the Presidio, where a long jump competition is in progress.

Soldiers steady a mule and caisson-mounted weaponry in the Presidio during World War I exercises.

THE INTERWAR YEARS

(1920–1938)

San Francisco entered the 1920s proud and confident. The decade of jazz and flappers was a paradoxical one, with innocence wedded to extravagance, avant-garde as much as it was conservative. Trends throughout the country became magnified to extremes in San Francisco's cultural lens, and as always, the city's population carried on in a grandiose and exceptional style. A sudden departure from the traditional and familiar to new technologies and ways of living marked the era. Many Americans experienced unprecedented prosperity and optimism for the future, while others experienced profound resistance, fear, and apprehension. The Presidio further expanded in this decade with the inauguration of Crissy Army Airfield as part of harbor defenses. In 1924, the first transcontinental flight ended its journey at this pioneering military airfield.

During the thirties, San Francisco plunged into the Great Depression along with the rest of the nation. San Franciscans were forced to make an abrupt shift, from the life-styles they led in the bountiful twenties to a frugal existence that allowed for none of the extravagances of the previous decade. Bread lines and soup kitchens suddenly became ubiquitous on San Francisco streets. Yet while the Great Depression was a dark moment in the city's history, San Franciscans had overcome adversity before. People pursued their lives as best they could. In many ways, entertainment was more accessible to the general public now, with many cheap diversions available throughout the city, such as Playland at the Beach, vaudevilles, theaters, and parks like the Presidio, which were opened for public recreation.

President Franklin D. Roosevelt's New Deal used government spending on a large scale to alleviate unemployment across the nation, which in San Francisco meant significant new construction projects. Among them were the Bay Bridge and Golden Gate Bridge, completed in 1936 and 1937, to become beloved landmarks and transform how people lived and worked, at last linking San Francisco to the East Bay and Marin County. From 1933 to 1937, during construction of the Golden Gate Bridge, the Presidio became a more popular public destination. New Deal public works projects also included restoring the Presidio Officers' Quarters in 1934, in mission revival style.

One of the cottages on Officers' Row served as the library and billiards room, a popular recreation activity for officers. This photograph of the billiards room was taken in the early 1920s.

Fort Point is shown here as it appeared on September 15, 1923, a dozen or so years before construction of the Golden Gate Bridge would begin to overshadow it.

The Officers' Club, shown here on September 15, 1923, was a private facility for the use of officers based at the Presidio. The Officers' Club and Mission Dolores are the only structures from the Spanish colonial era in San Francisco to survive. Built in 1776, this was the original Commandant Quarters when the Presidio and the city were under Spanish rule. The structure was remodeled many times after it was built, including in 1850 and 1900. In 1912, electricity was installed, and in 1934, under President Franklin Roosevelt's New Deal programs, the club was renovated once again, this time in mission revival style. The front walls of the club, which are original to the eighteenth-century Spanish fort, remain intact, and numerous artifacts from the Spanish period have been excavated in the area.

This aerial view of the Golden Gate, Fort Point, and Crissy Field was photographed around 1920. Crissy Airfield was built by the military at the Presidio to develop the military usefulness of airplanes. Completed in 1921 and named for Major Dana H. Crissy, an aviator who died during flight in 1919, it was the first military Air Coast Defense Station on the West Coast. During the interwar period, innovations in aviation developed at stations like Crissy Field would help the Allies win World War II.

Young children stretch out arm-to-arm in front of the wing of a plane at Crissy Field in the early 1920s. San Francisco native Lincoln Beachey performed impressive air stunts to cheering crowds at the Panama-Pacific International Exposition over what would soon become Crissy Field. He was the first pilot to fly a plane upside down, and to successfully pull off a spin recovery and tail slide. Beachey, a fearless pilot and adventurer, ultimately died while performing for crowds. The wings collapsed in a monoplane he was flying, and he drowned in the Bay between Crissy Field and Fort Mason as spectators watched helplessly.

The children enjoy the tarmac view from atop the biplane's wings. The fog and wind, vulnerability to enemy planes because of its ocean-side locale, and the building of the Golden Gate Bridge led to the closing of Crissy Field as an air base in 1936. In subsequent years, especially during the Second World War, the hangars and warehouses of Crissy Field were used as an assembly spot for troops, and for offices and other purposes, including the top-secret Military Intelligence Language School for Nisei soldiers.

Young future pilots measure themselves against two bombs in Crissy Field in the early 1920s. This image comes from the Brett Photo Album, which is part of the Dora Devol Brett Collection of historic photos.

Five planes in close formation are pictured at an aerial flying circus at Crissy Field on Saturday, April 28, 1924, which was attended by nearly all personnel of the Army post.

Two men examine the tents on Army Day in the Presidio during the 1920s.

Checker taxi drivers, members of Motor Transport Company (Reserve), are being drilled
by army officers at the Presidio on July 3, 1925.

A formation of the 91st Squadron flies over the Presidio in the 1920s.

A military ceremony is held at the Monument to the Unknown Soldier at the Presidio on May 30, 1931.

This photograph taken in June 1931 in front of the Montgomery Street Barracks shows First Sergeant Shramar of the 30th Infantry Regiment instructing his daughter in the use of this Browning .30 caliber machine gun. The 30th Infantry was nicknamed "San Francisco's Own."

This photograph, taken on October 17, 1930, by the U.S. Army Air Corps, provides an aerial view of the Presidio grounds. At center is Crissy Field, on the left is the Post of the Presidio, in the background Fort Winfield Scott, at left-center the Palace of Fine Arts, and at upper-right is Fort Point, with the Pacific Ocean beyond.

This striking three-story building is the old Wright Army Hospital, built in 1864 during the Civil War and shown here in the 1930s. It was designed as an Italianate and Greek-revival structure. After the hospital closed in 1897, the building was used for many years to provide medical and dental services to soldiers. Between 1974 and February 2001, the building housed the Presidio Army Museum. Cannons and other weaponry can still be seen on the grounds of this building.

On April 9, 1931, near the Presidio stables, a soldier is working through technical difficulties related to regimental defense.

88

Four soldiers examine the target on an archery field at the Presidio on August 17, 1932. Two bull's-eyes suggest skilled marksmanship among these soldiers.

Twin-engine bombers fly over Crissy Field on February 9, 1933. The city of San Francisco rises in the background.

Construction on the Golden Gate Bridge began January 5, 1933. This picture taken on March 3 shows bridge construction at Fort Point, two months after the project began. Between 1933 and 1937 when the bridge was completed, 11 men were killed when they fell during construction, 10 of them only because safety netting failed. The small number of accidents was testimony to the emphasis Joseph Strauss, the man in charge of the project, had placed on safety.

Golden Gate Bridge
construction workers eat
cafeteria-style at Fort Point
on March 7, 1933.

Trained fire fighters based at the Presidio Fire Station are pictured here on April 26, 1933, standing on the running boards of one of their fire engines parked in front of the station built in 1917. In 1933, the Presidio Fire Department was managed by Sergeant W. M. Williams.

Sergeant M. Camino of the 76th Field Artillery is photographed on April 6, 1934, as he walks a pair of horses.

Spectators watch as troops march during Army Day festivities in the Presidio on April 7, 1934.

Admiral Senn, General Craig, Mayor Rossi, Jesse Coleman, and Alfred Cleary are shown attending Army Day in the Presidio on April 12, 1934.

Soldiers watch the San Francisco Traffic Police School on the Parade Grounds at the Presidio on April 27, 1934.

Members of the San Francisco Junior Traffic Patrol are pictured marching through the Presidio on May 29, 1935.

Soldiers of the 30th Infantry are shown marching at the Presidio on May 16, 1935.

Marguerite Barnett and Irene Palladini work on a scale model of the Presidio in 1936. The model was a Federal Art Project undertaking for the Junior Chamber of Commerce, and was formally presented to Colonel I. J. Phillipson, commanding officer of the 30th Infantry at a luncheon held in the Palace Hotel on Tuesday, December 8, 1936. The FAP was one of Roosevelt's many New Deal programs aimed at steering Americans through the Great Depression. The Lombard Street Gate is seen just below Miss Barnett's forearm. In the background is the official contour map from which the model was made.

Privates Ellis Thorpe, J. W. Warney, Al Boss, and Eugene Peckham place flowers at a grave site at the Presidio National Cemetery on Memorial Day, May 30, 1936.

Corporal B. G. Byrd is showing three young boys an old mortar at the Presidio on June 8, 1936.

A group of women, Betty Collins, Isabella Henry, Barbara Jones, Doradell Meredith, Polly Willard, Evangeline Barnes, Doris Henry, and Kathleen Nye, pose on an airplane wing at Crissy Field on April 2, 1937.

Following Spread: A review of troops takes place at the Presidio on June 30, 1937.

The Presidio's R. G. Barren hillsides bloom in brilliant color in 1939 thanks to Madison School students who undertook a weeding and planting project as part of a campaign to beautify the city in preparation for the influx of visitors to the World Exposition of 1939. A group of the students are shown getting instructions from R. G. Milani, Director of Gardens for the school department.

The military funeral procession for Colonel John T. Nance took place at the Presidio on April 23, 1938. Colonel Nance was in the 9th Cavalry and served in China and the Philippines, later becoming a Professor of Military Tactics.

Sergeant David Gillimer is pictured here with three members of the San Francisco Junior
Traffic Patrol on October 28, 1938.

THE WORLD WAR II YEARS

(1939–1945)

While the nations of Europe and Asia were deeply involved in war in 1939, the United States remained neutral. On December 7, 1941, with the Japanese attack at Pearl Harbor, San Francisco was transformed from a city blissfully isolated from the crises abroad into the subject of worldwide attention.

Within hours of the news from Hawaii, the city declared an official state of emergency and citizens were forced to quickly adapt to wartime. Public figures united the community, and military officials began aggressive campaigns to rid the area of anyone who could pose a threat from within. As the city mobilized to serve as a central port of supplies for and embarkation to the Pacific theater, citizens grew intensely patriotic, raising money for war bonds and participating in rationings.

The Presidio served as the headquarters for the Western Defense Command during the war, and nearly two million men embarked from Fort Mason to fight in the Pacific. More soldiers returned to the Presidio than to any other base in the United States, and Letterman Hospital admitted 72,000 patients during a single year. As the Western Defense Command, the Presidio had the profound duty of defending the entire West Coast and once again filled with temporary encampments and training facilities for the war. Soldiers hollowed foxholes into the beaches. Trainloads of wounded soldiers and casualties from Okinawa and Iwo Jima were brought to be treated at the hospital.

When President Franklin Roosevelt signed Executive Order 9066 on February 19, 1942, John L. DeWitt, the commanding general of the Western Defense Command, oversaw the internment of more than 100,000 persons of Japanese ancestry, two-thirds of whom were American born. American soldiers of Japanese descent were trained to speak and read the Japanese language at the Military Intelligence Service Language School in Crissy Field to be interpreters and code breakers. Paradoxically, the families of some of these soldiers were themselves interned.

It took the war to finally shake the country out of the Great Depression. The war created millions of jobs, many of them, especially shipbuilding, based in the San Francisco Bay Area. When the war ended in 1945, San Francisco hosted the U.N. World Charter of Security. A committee visited the Presidio to consider it as a future headquarters for the United Nations.

San Francisco mayor Angelo J. Rossi, in office from 1933 to 1944, is shown delivering a Memorial Day address at the Presidio's Monument to the Unknown Soldier, May 30, 1939.

Pictured here is a coastal defense gun at Fort Winfield Scott on September 27, 1939. Fort Scott, opened in the western quarter of the Presidio on June 19, 1912, was the coast artillery garrison and headquarters of the artillery district of the city. It had 17 gun batteries in operation between 1891 and 1946. In 1922, Fort Scott became the headquarters of the Coast Defenses of San Francisco (renamed Harbor Defenses in 1925) and controlled the other forts in the Bay Area, including Fort Baker and Fort Funston. The fort was named in honor of General Winfield Scott, a hero of the Mexican War and a commander of the Union Army early in the Civil War. Fort Point was originally known as Fort Winfield Scott, from 1882 to 1886.

A group of U.S. senators and congressmen is pictured standing at Crissy Field on December 2, 1939. Shown from left to right are General Henry T. Burgin Minton, Senator Elmer Thomas, Representative John Sparkman, Senator John Chandler "Chan" Gurney, Senator Dennis Chavez, Senator Harry Truman, Representative William D. Byron, Representative Charles R. Clasow, Representative Paul W. Shafer, Representative Overton Brooks, Representative John M. Costello, and Representative Thomas E. Martin.

Against cypress trees at the Presidio National Cemetery, an Armistice Day salute is fired to America's war dead on November 11, 1940. The 28-acre San Francisco National Cemetery was founded in 1884 and is the final resting place of more than 30,000 people, from the Civil War to the present, including 35 winners of the Congressional Medal of Honor, and nearly 500 Buffalo Soldiers. Among the graves of illustrious Americans here is that of General Frederick Funston, hero of the Spanish-American War who captured Emilio Aguinaldo and took charge of the recovery of the city after the 1906 earthquake.

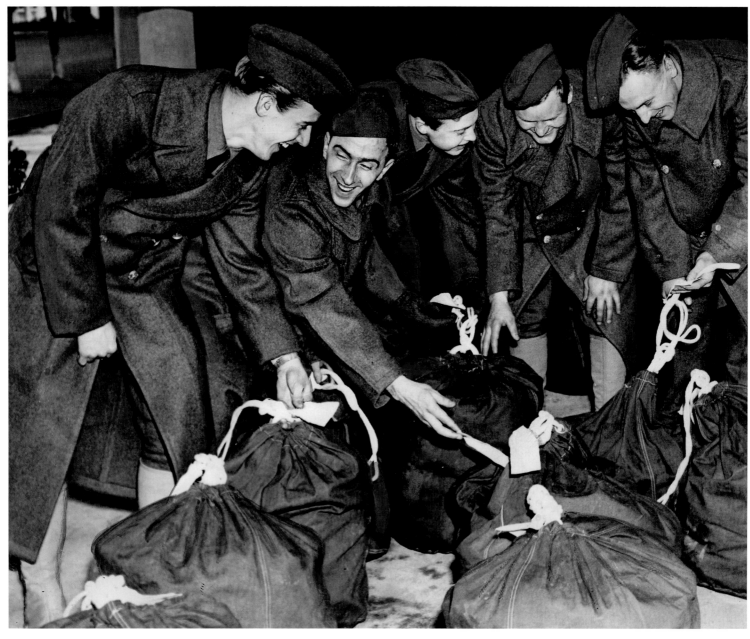

Soldiers on their way to Fort Winfield Scott in the Presidio are shown arriving in Oakland from the Midwest on January 25, 1941. The soldiers are seen identifying their duffle bags prior to their assignments at Fort Barry and Fort Scott.

Members of the 30th Infantry stand at ease during a review at Crissy Field in the Presidio on March 15, 1941, as the regiment parades. More than half the men were recent inductees. The review was highlighted with the presentation of chevrons to 275 of the infantrymen, dressed in full combat uniform.

Trucks from the 30th Infantry at the Presidio and the 32nd Infantry at Fort Ord transfer 800 soldiers. Seen in the background is the Palace of Fine Arts, built for the Panama-Pacific International Exposition in 1915.

Soldiers lift a new military jeep at Crissy Field early in the war years for an inspection. The jeep was being prepared for military traffic duty in the Presidio. The majestic Golden Gate Bridge, completed a few years earlier, rises in the background.

Troops are shown arriving at the Presidio by bus early in the war years.

Soldiers line up dozens of jeeps at Crissy Field. Beyond is the Golden Gate Bridge, and beyond that is the Pacific Ocean, destination of the many recruits soon to arrive at the Presidio.

Following Spread: 30th Infantry troops are pictured marching in the Presidio early in the war.

Soldiers get Red Cross first-aid training at the Presidio.

A soldier parks himself in a "no parking" zone in the early years of World War II.

Temporary crew quarters, with projectiles stacked in the right rear at Battery Chamberlin, are pictured here in July 1942. Situated at the northern end of the Baker Beach parking lot, this battery (named in honor of Lowell Chamberlin, a distinguished Civil War artillery officer) was part of a system of coastal defenses built between the 1880s and 1910s. It was completed in 1904, and included four 6-inch guns with a range of up to eight miles at two rounds per minute. These guns were removed for use during the First World War. During the Second World War, many feared an imminent attack by Japan on the Golden Gate, and Battery Chamberlin served a central role in coastal defense.

Shown here is an Armistice Day ceremony at the Presidio in the early 1940s.

Battery Chamberlin, shown here in 1942, was manned by the Sixth Coast Artillery Regiment, Battery D.

War preparedness at Battery Chamberlin is under way in the fall of 1942. The guns used at the battery were camouflaged with netting and sat on disappearing platforms, to give the crew and guns protection behind a concrete shield during loading and unloading. Soldiers stationed here waited for an enemy that never came. During the war, an ammunition storage room served as a cramped barracks. The new military technology of World War II would leave the old battery coastal defense system obsolete, especially during the cold war era of missiles and atomic weapons to follow. In 1948, the batteries were disarmed.

Pictured here in 1942 are the temporary crew quarters at Fort Winfield Scott.

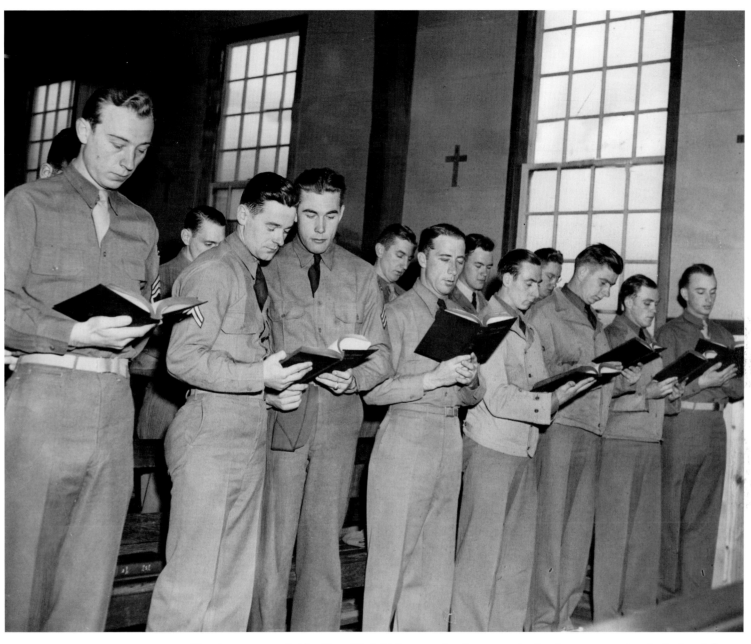

Church services are held at Fort Winfield Scott on October 31, 1942, for the men manning the harbor defenses.

A group of boys gathers in 1942 around military equipment displayed in the Presidio.

The Guard of Honor participates in Armistice Day ceremonies at the San Francisco National Cemetery on November 11, 1942.

Soldiers study at Crissy Field at the Military Intelligence Service Language School. From the late 1930s forward, it became clear that the United States might have to go to war with Japan. The U.S. Army prepared for this in part by establishing the 4th Army Intelligence School in November 1941 at Crissy Field. During World War II, some 120,000 persons of Japanese descent or ethnicity were removed to 19 internment camps on orders issuing from the Main Post in the Presidio, out of concern that those with close ties to Japan could pose a threat to national security. The hardships imposed by this action did not deter many Americans of Japanese ancestry from enlisting in the services and fighting with honor overseas.

Nisei interpreters focus on their studies in a Japanese language class in the language school at Crissy Field. This top-secret school trained a total of 60 American soldiers (58 of whom were of Japanese descent) to speak and read Japanese, with the objective to become interpreters and code breakers in the war. The school convened in a converted hangar thought by civilians and other military personnel to be a laundry house. These students were involved in a one-year training program, condensed into half a year after the bombing of Pearl Harbor. The school's curriculum was very difficult—by April 1942, only 44 of the students had successfully completed their training. Shortly afterward, the school was relocated to a military base in Minnesota.

A group of female Nisei interpreters examine documents during the war. These Nisei soldiers were deployed to the major battle sites in the Pacific theater, serving an important role in code-breaking, translating stolen documents, and interrogating prisoners of war, as well as in the American postwar occupation of Japan. It has been said that the efforts of these Nisei soldiers saved countless Allied lives.

A casualty drill at Letterman General Hospital on April 22, 1943, is under way here. At regular intervals, officers and enlisted personnel at Letterman simulated caring for the wounded under actual combat conditions.

A Memorial Day service is held at the Monument to the Unknown Soldier on May 31, 1943. Many of the civilians and families at this service have lost loved ones in battle. This ceremony followed the Memorial Day parade along Lombard Street and dedication of Gold Star markers.

Letterman Army Medical Center nurses receive pins for their war service from a Presidio officer.

Servicemen enjoy a snack at the Presidio canteen in 1943.

This group of soldiers is engaged in a tug of war in the Presidio on August 31, 1943.

Generals, admirals, and others are shown at a Presidio banquet held in 1944.

A soldier wounded in service receives a medal during ceremonies at Letterman General Hospital.

The Citizens Committee, civic leaders, Army officials, representatives of veterans organizations, members of the French delegation to a security conference, and other San Franciscans gather for services at the National Cemetery in the Presidio.

Service personnel gaze toward the Pacific from Battery Chamberlin in 1945. Fort Point and the heart of the Presidio lie toward the Golden Gate Bridge, beyond the grove of conifers at right.

Soldiers check in and fill out paperwork at Letterman Army Medical Center in the Presidio at the end of the war.

THE POSTWAR YEARS

(1946–1970s)

With the end of World War II, amid the jubilation of the Allied victory, tens of thousands of soldiers returned home to the Bay Area, many to attend college for the first time under the G.I. Bill. In 1946, the command at the Presidio was renamed the Sixth U.S. Army and charged once again with training, supplying, and deploying army forces in the American West, as well as coordinating disaster relief.

By the 1950s, America was fully enmeshed in the cold war against the Soviet Union. During the Korean War, the Presidio once again came into action as military headquarters, and Letterman Hospital prepared to care for the injured. The Presidio continued to play a key role as well in the nation's increasing involvement in the Pacific Rim. In 1951, the ANZUS Treaty was signed at the reservation, a pact of security between the United States, Australia, and New Zealand. That same year, the Japan-U.S. security treaty was signed here. During this time, the Presidio served as the center of operations for Nike missile defense, which was positioned all over the Golden Gate, as well as the base for the eminent Sixth U.S. Army.

The Presidio was declared a National Historic Landmark in 1962. In the 1960s, the country found itself fiercely divided over the Vietnam War and civil rights. The civil rights movement fundamentally changed social relations in America. San Francisco's youth rebelled against the established order, causing general social upheaval. The Presidio played a role in the Vietnam War, and war protestors held anti-war demonstrations at the Presidio gates. In 1968, a prisoner at the Presidio stockade named Michael Bunch was shot while trying to escape, initiating the Presidio Mutiny, a protest among 27 prisoners.

Sweeping changes would occur in the status of the Presidio in the coming decades. Between 1969 and 1974, the Letterman Army Hospital was renovated, and the Letterman Army Institute of Research was established. In 1972, the Golden Gate National Recreation Area was established, and it was determined that should the Presidio no longer be required by the military, it would become part of the GGNRA. In 1989, the army closed the Presidio as a military base. In 1991, the remaining units of the Sixth Army were deployed for war for the last time to fight in Desert Storm, the first Persian Gulf War. In 1994, the Sixth Army became inactive, and the Presidio was placed under the control of the National Park Service as part of the Golden Gate National Recreation Area, beginning a new era in the history of this important landmark.

Jesse M. Nichols is shown standing with a turkey at Fort Point. The unlucky bird fell into San Francisco Bay but was rescued by a Coast Guard crash boat.

Stilwell Hall is shown here on June 12, 1947. The three-story building housed troops, schools, unit headquarters, and officers' clubs of the California-Nevada Organized Reserves at the Presidio. The structure overhead is the southern approach to the Golden Gate Bridge. Stilwell Hall was so-named in memory of the late four-star General Joseph W. Stilwell, who led Allied forces in China and Burma during World War II. Stilwell was nicknamed "Vinegar Joe" for his harsh methods as a commander and "Uncle Joe" because of his concern for the average soldier.

Fort Point is pictured here on April 9, 1948. The spans of the Golden Gate Bridge in this area were designed to mesh architecturally with the fort.

An Armistice Day ceremony at the San Francisco National Cemetery on November 11, 1948, honors the men who died in World War I.

The Sixth Army Headquarters Building of the Presidio is pictured here on December 22, 1948. The morning's heavy frost provided a setting reminiscent of the snowbound East.

The San Francisco Port of Embarkation Band, pictured in rehearsal here on April 21, 1949, was to perform in a concert three days later.

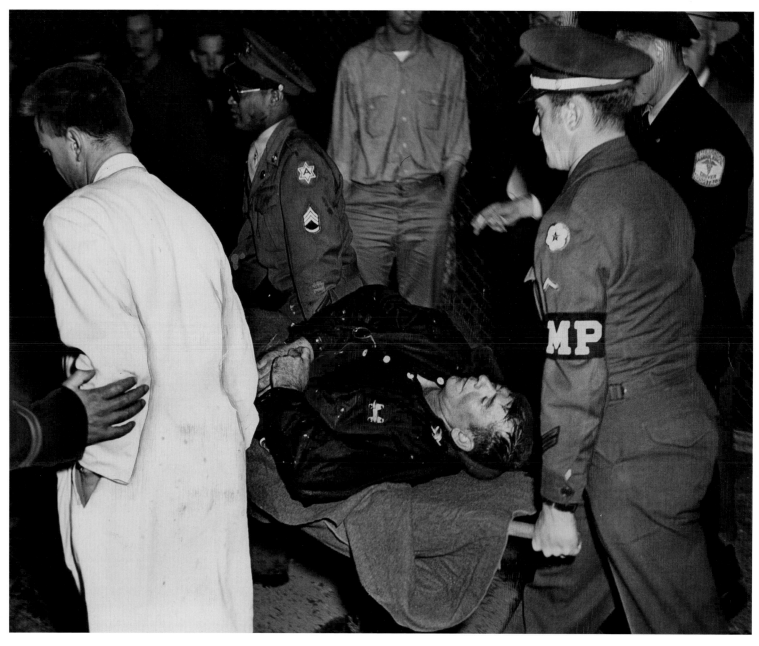

Fireman Ovid Seyler is carried to an ambulance by army personnel on September 30, 1948. He was overcome by smoke while fighting a fire which destroyed a Presidio warehouse.

The Presidio Post Chapel, shown here on March 9, 1949, was a favorite place for weddings—1,260 couples were married beneath the high-beamed ceiling of this Spanish mission revival–style chapel since 1931, the year it opened. Protestant services, including children's Sunday school and youth vespers, were also held here, with regular services into the mid-1990s. It is now an interfaith chapel open to the public. A beautiful depression-era mural in the chapel, painted by Victor Mikhail Arnautoff in 1934, graces the east wall. It depicts army peacetime activities, as well as important historical figures and a famous love story in Presidio history. Maria de la Concepcion Marcela Arguello, born in the Presidio in 1791, was engaged at the age of 15 to Nikolai Rezanov, a much older Russian Chamberlain who visited the Presidio. Because both Spain and Russia were attempting to establish hegemony in California, Maria's parents considered the marriage politically beneficial. The story ended tragically for Maria when Rezanov went back to Europe and died of illness, never returning to his betrothed.

Naval Harbor Defense students join Army students in 1949 to study submarine mining operations at the Seacoast Artillery School at Fort Winfield Scott.

On January 23, 1950, Captain S. L. Piersall of the 701st Military Police Battalion at the Presidio shows students proper firing procedures for military funerals.

Students of a joint Army-Navy military police school are pictured at the Lombard Gate entrance to the Presidio. At left is Corporal Thomas Wilson of the Oakland Army Base and at right is Loren H. Caughran of the Navy of San Francisco. Caughran hailed from Knoxville, Tennessee, and Wilson from Redwood City, California. Both were attending the school's joint services course to learn military police and shore patrol procedures.

Pictured here are members of the 65-piece Sixth Army Official Band of the Presidio performing on August 3, 1950.

Shown in this photograph is a gun crew of Battery C 60th Anti-Aircraft Artillery Battalion at Fort Scott. The crew was tracking a National Guard B-26, flying low over the Golden Gate Bridge, as part of a training exercise on September 21, 1950. The plane was piloted by Lieutenant H. E. Hartwig, stationed at San Jose.

The Presidio Fire Station is pictured here decorated for Christmas on December 21, 1950. Not interested in ranking second-best against other fire departments, station personnel spared no effort.

Following Spread: A new flagpole is being transported to the Presidio at the Lombard Street entrance. This was the city's largest flagpole, measuring 115 feet and 6 inches, and weighing in at 2.5 tons. Once installed, the pole stood anchored 10 feet into the ground, and flew a garrison flag measuring 20 by 38 feet.

El Polin Springs is shown here in 1951. In 1898, the First Tennessee Volunteer Infantry Regiment camped here during the Spanish-American War. In the early days of the Presidio, native people relied on the fresh water abundant in the area from Mountain Lake, El Polin Springs, and Lobos Creek. El Polin once provided fresh water to the Presidio, and Spanish and Mexican colonial families made their homes here. An ongoing archaeological study of El Polin Springs by Stanford University, in partnership with the National Park Service and the Presidio Trust, seeks to understand how this valley was used under Spanish and Mexican Rule, between 1776 and 1847, and the interactions among the diverse communities living here at the time. In summer 2003, the stone foundation of an early nineteenth century adobe house, that of the Briones family, was discovered in the southern part of the Tennessee Hollow. The Briones family figured importantly in San Francisco in the Spanish and Mexican periods.

On May 19, 1951, San Franciscans attend an open house celebrating Armed Forces Day on the Presidio's parade grounds. All branches of the Armed Forces demonstrated equipment and skills to visitors during the afternoon. Bob Warren of the News Camera Staff took this photo from an Air Force helicopter.

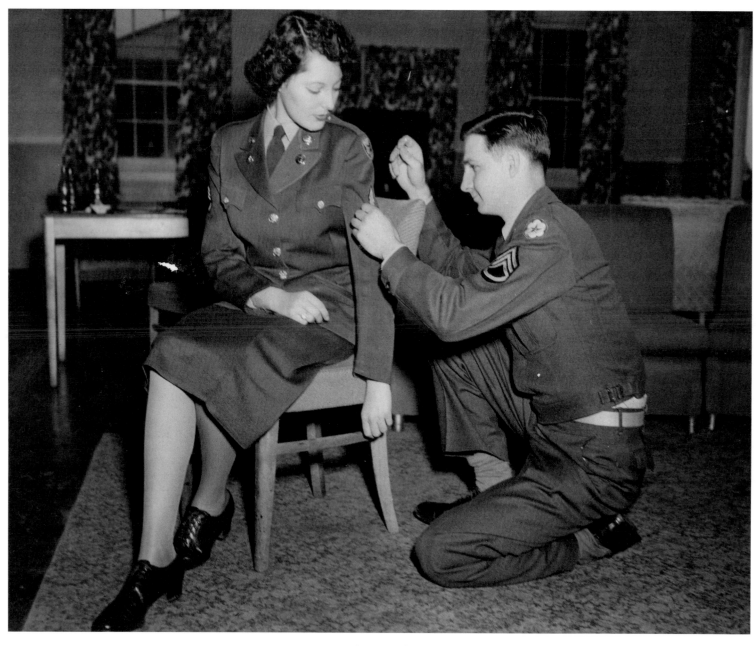

An NCO (Non-Commissioned Officer) sews stripes on the sleeves of another at
Letterman Hospital on March 6, 1951.

Civilian visitors are shown sampling army food on Armed Forces Day at the Presidio on May 21, 1951.
Crowds of visitors got to taste "army chow" in a mess hall as the Presidio opened its doors in observance of
Armed Forces Day and I Am an American Day. A picture on the back wall depicts Old Faithful, the famous
geyser at Yellowstone Park.

Soldiers are shown here servicing a 120 mm anti-aircraft gun at the Presidio in 1951. The Korean War was then in progress.

The Sixth Army Pipe Band is pictured in front of the Enlisted Service Club in the Presidio on May 14, 1952. This colorful band, known as the "Kilties," provided music on Armed Forces Day in Lakeside Park, Oakland. The eight pipers, four drummers, and their mascot combined to form the only military bagpipe band in the area.

This panorama of the Presidio environs includes Alcatraz Island, in the background at right, and the Palace of Fine Arts, the domed structure at left, as they appeared in the early 1950s.

Captain Doris M. Mertof of the Women's Army Corps poses for the photographer in 1952 at Crissy Field.

A "junior fireman" blows out a match in the Presidio in 1952 while another looks on.

Military personnel at the Presidio make last-minute preparations for Armed Forces Day 1952 as they set up exhibits to be shown to civilian spectators during the all-day open house.

This December 1953 image, from the Letterman Technician's Scrapbook, shows a Presidio nutrition lab, where Captain Glaskowsky and others are on tour.

Presidio soldiers are shown reading in a library in 1953. Shipments of books, fiction and nonfiction, were occasionally sent to troops serving on the front line in Korea.

A soldier and a young patient are reading together at the Letterman Hospital in the 1950s.

Pictured here is the Sixth Army Flight Detachment at Crissy Field in 1955.

This aerial view of the Presidio from October 1955 encompasses the reservation in relation to other segments of San Francisco. The Bay Bridge is in the background, and behind it, under a layer of fog, is Oakland. The island the bridge traverses is Yerba Buena, and to the left of the island is Treasure Island, a U.S. naval base during and after World War II. As a result of the western-bound trend in population and industrial growth, the mild climate of San Francisco, and the growing importance of the Pacific in international relations, there was talk among those in Washington, D.C., proposing an alternate capital in San Francisco and a "Western White House."

Golf enthusiasts enjoy the Presidio golf course in the 1950s.

Troops bound ashore on May 15, 1956, in dress rehearsal for an Armed Forces Day amphibious landing at the Presidio.

An audience attends beach-landing activities to witness the "frogman operation" on Armed Forces Day in 1956.

Kim Yong Woo, Korean Minister of National Defense, is greeted by Colonel H. A. Davenport and other dignitaries at the Presidio on April 4, 1957.

The Army Nurse's Corps of Letterman Hospital celebrates its 56th anniversary on February 2, 1957.

This is an aerial view of the Marine Hospital as it appeared in January 1959.

Waves crash against the seawall at Fort Point on February 8, 1960, as this woman looks on. A terrible storm with torrential downpours and gale force winds brought minor flooding to many parts of the Bay Area, as well as fallen trees and power lines, car accidents, and widespread blackouts.

An officer in the control tower at Crissy Field surveys the skies around San Francisco Bay in 1960.

Citizens examine the defenses in the Presidio during Armed Forces Day in May 1960. This surveillance drone was among the armaments exhibited that year. Radio-controlled, drones of this kind could carry a 90-pound payload of camera surveillance equipment to targets within a range of 50 miles.

On Armed Forces Day in the Presidio on May 21, 1960, the Army air defense "Nike in Action" missiles are on display. The Presidio was a center of Nike missile development during the cold war. At that time, the U.S. was worried about the threat of foreign attack by aircraft carrying nuclear weapons. Between the Korean War and 1972, when the Strategic Arms Limitation Treaty was signed, Nike anti-aircraft defenses based at sites in the San Francisco area, including at Fort Winfield Scott, were kept at a high state of preparedness. By the 1970s, newer defense technologies replaced the obsolete Nike missiles, and all of the Nike facilities in the Bay Area except the one at nearby Fort Barry were dismantled.

Young boys inspect a U.S. Army jeep during Armed Forces Day.

Following Spread: Four young Americans demonstrate their rifle skills at Armed Forces Day in the Presidio on May 21, 1960.

A woman poses on the steps of a U.S. Army Special Services bookmobile in 1960.

This Presidio U.S. Army helicopter hovers over the Golden Gate Bridge on July 18, 1961. The Presidio grounds are visible in the background, on the far side of the bridge.

This photograph shows the West Coast World War II Memorial to the Missing with a statue of Columbia and a list of those lost or buried at sea in the Pacific theater. The monument stands amid cypress and Monterey pine trees overlooking the Pacific Ocean. It was dedicated on November 29, 1960, with the names of 413 soldiers from all branches of the service.

Members of the Northern Area Command State Military Reserve are planning "Operation Pandora" in Fort Scott in the Presidio, on May 23 and 24, 1964. This exercise was designed to test state troops in their mission to assist civil government in emergencies.

Shown here in the 1960s is the "brain" of the Sixth Army's Communications center. This was a top-secret room, and anyone entering it needed to have security clearance. Teletypes were linked directly with Army, Navy, and Air Defense headquarters at Colorado Springs, Colorado.

Shown here is the demolition of the old wards at Letterman Hospital on July 20, 1965, as work began to clear the way for a new 550-bed structure on the site of the old. Congress had appropriated $13.7 million toward the project. A bulldozer rips into the old ward adjoining the main building at Letterman, as workers put water on the debris to keep the dust down. At right a video photographer records the event.

One of the architectural anomalies of the Presidio, the Log Cabin, is shown here at Fort Winfield Scott in the early 1970s, with downtown San Francisco rising in the background. In 1962, the Presidio was designated a National Historic Landmark District for its historical significance from 1776 to 1945. Many buildings had been altered, especially as military structures were transformed for new purposes in peacetime. Under the National Historic Preservation Act, historically significant buildings are being preserved.

Shown here in the early 1970s is a general exterior view of the Old Wright Station Hospital at Funston Avenue and Lincoln Boulevard.

Soldiers march with flags in 1976 at a Bicentennial celebration parade at the Presidio.

A volunteer with the Fort Point Museum Association sports period uniform inside Fort Point.

Notes on the Photographs

These notes, listed by page number, attempt to include all aspects known of the photographs. Each of the photographs is identified by the page number, photograph's title or description, photographer and collection, archive, and call or box number when applicable. Although every attempt was made to collect all data, in some cases complete data may have been unavailable due to the age and condition of some of the photographs and records.

123 **PARKED SOLDIER**
Courtesy Golden Gate NRA,
Park Archives,
Leo Ghilardi Collection
GOGA-2497

124 **BATTERY CHAMBERLIN CREW QUARTERS**
Courtesy Golden Gate NRA,
Park Archives,
PAM Prints Collection,
GOGA-1766

125 **ARMISTICE DAY CEREMONIES 1940S**
San Francisco History Center,
San Francisco Public Library
AAC-0457

126 **BATTERY CHAMBERLIN 1942**
Courtesy Golden Gate NRA,
Park Archives,
PAM Prints Collection,
GOGA-35256.0613

127 **BATTERY CHAMBERLIN CAMOUFLAGE**
Courtesy Golden Gate NRA,
Park Archives,
PAM Negative Collection,
GOGA-1766

128 **QUARTERS AT FORT WINFIELD SCOTT**
Courtesy Golden Gate NRA,
Park Archives,
PAM Prints Collection,
GOGA-1766

129 **FORT SCOTT CHURCH SERVICES**
San Francisco History Center,
San Francisco Public Library
AAC-1009

130 **MILITARY EQUIPMENT DISPLAY 1942**
Courtesy Golden Gate NRA,
Park Archives,
PAM Prints Collection
GOGA-1766

131 **ARMISTICE DAY GUARD OF HONOR**
Courtesy Golden Gate NRA,
Park Archives,
PAM Prints Collection
GOGA-1766

132 **WORLD WAR II INTELLIGENCE LANGUAGE SCHOOL**
Courtesy Golden Gate NRA,
Park Archives,
Crissy Field History Study Collection,
GOGA-2255

133 **INTELLIGENCE LANGUAGE SCHOOL 2**
Courtesy Golden Gate NRA,
Park Archives,
TASC Negative Collection,
GOGA-35301.3223

134 **NISEI INTERPRETERS**
Courtesy Golden Gate NRA,
Park Archives,
TASC Negative Collection,
GOGA-35301.3224

135 **CASUALTY DRILL AT LETTERMAN HOSPITAL**
San Francisco History Center,
San Francisco Public Library
AAD-0240

136 **MEMORIAL DAY SERVICE 1943**
San Francisco History Center,
San Francisco Public Library
AAC-1213

137 **CEREMONY FOR LETTERMAN NURSES**
Courtesy Golden Gate NRA,
Park Archives,
TASC Negative Collection,
GOGA-35301.1815

138 **PRESIDIO CANTEEN**
Courtesy Golden Gate NRA,
Park Archives,
PAM Prints Collection
GOGA-1766

139 **TUG OF WAR 1943**
San Francisco History Center,
San Francisco Public Library
AAC-0898

140 **PRESIDIO BANQUET**
Courtesy Golden Gate NRA,
Park Archives,
General Ralph E. Haines Papers,
GOGA-35313.123

141 **AWARD FOR WOUNDED SOLDIER**
San Francisco History Center,
San Francisco Public Library
AAD-0225

142 **NATIONAL CEMETERY SERVICES**
San Francisco History Center,
San Francisco Public Library
AAC-0857

143 **BATTERY CHAMBERLIN GUN**
Courtesy Golden Gate NRA,
Park Archives,
Interpretation Negative Coll.
GOGA-2316

144 **END OF WORLD WAR II PAPERWORK**
Courtesy Golden Gate NRA,
Park Archives,
Letterman Army Med. Center Photo File
GOGA-35288

146 **GOLDEN GATE TURKEY**
San Francisco History Center,
San Francisco Public Library
AAC-0933

147 **STILWELL HALL 1947**
San Francisco History Center,
San Francisco Public Library
AAC-1179

148 **GOLDEN GATE BRIDGE AT FORT POINT**
San Francisco History Center,
San Francisco Public Library
AAC-0928

149 **ARMISTICE DAY 1948**
San Francisco History Center,
San Francisco Public Library
AAD-6225

150 **SIXTH ARMY HEADQUARTERS**
San Francisco History Center,
San Francisco Public Library
AAC-1172

151 **PORT OF EMBARKATION BAND AT HEADQUARTERS**
San Francisco History Center,
San Francisco Public Library
AAC-1168

152 **INJURED FIRE FIGHTER**
San Francisco History Center,
San Francisco Public Library
AAC-0984